LOOK INSIDE

A VICTORIAN TOYSHOP

BRIAN MOSES
Illustrated by Adam Hook

WAYLAND

Editor: Jason Hook
Series design: Ian Winton
Book design: Heather Blackham
Cover design: Dennis Day

First published in 1997 by Wayland Publishers Ltd,
61 Western Road, Hove, East Sussex BN3 1JD, England
© Copyright 1997 Wayland Publishers Ltd.
Wayland are on the internet at http://www.wayland.co.uk

British Library Cataloguing in Publication Data
Moses, Brian, 1950-
   Look inside a Victorian Toyshop
   1. Toys - Great Britain - History - 19th century -
Juvenile literature 2. Great Britain - Social life and
customs - 19th century - Juvenile literature
   I. Title II. Hook, Adam III. A Victorian Toyshop
   688. 7'2'0941

ISBN 0 7502 1997 1

Printed and bound in Italy by G. Canale & CSpA, Turin.
Colour reproduction by Page Turn, Hove, England.

Cover: A still from *Scrooge* (1970) (centre); mechanical
zebra cart (top); spinning top (left); toy train (right).

Picture Acknowledgements
The publishers would like to thank the following for
permission to reproduce their pictures (t=top; c=centre;
b=bottom; l=left; r=right). All pictures are from the
Robert Opie collection, except: Beamish, North of
England Open Air Museum 15t; Bridgeman Art
Library/Fine Art Society 4bl, /Bethnal Green Museum
10b, 11b; Edinburgh Museum of Childhood 9cl, 16t; Mary
Evans 4br, 5, 8t, 19t, 20b, 21t, 21br; Ronald Grant *cover*
c; Hulton Getty 6c, 7b, 10t, 12b 13cl, 14c, 28b; Museum
of London *cover* t, 16c, 17b; Norfolk Museums Service
cover l, *cover* r, 4t, 14b, 17t, 27b, 28t, 30t; Pollocks Toy
Museum 22b; Victoria and Albert Museum 18b; Wayland
Picture Library 25t.

CONTENTS

TOYSHOP

THE SHOP WINDOW

It is December and Christmas is fast approaching. The Lowther Arcade in London is full of toyshops, each bursting at the seams with different toys. There are so many toys that they overflow into the crowded street. One group of children push through the bustling shoppers to gaze in wonder at the most magical toyshop window.

▲ A selection of Victorian toys.

Arranged on the pavement outside a Victorian toyshop were rows of dolls, rocking horses, drums, model yachts and children's teasets. There were toys from France, Germany and Switzerland, as well as those made by the shopkeeper himself. Over 1,200 different types of toys were listed in an early nineteenth-century shopping catalogue.

▲ Tempted by the toyshop window.

▶ A poem celebrating the Lowther Arcade.

The Lowther Arcade

TELL me, rosy little boy,
Listen, little maiden, too,
Do you love a fine new toy?
Yes, you say, of course you do.
Then your thought to Mother tell,
And she'll take her little maid,
And her little boy as well,
To this wonderful Arcade.

Active apes that climb up sticks,
Swords and guns and trumpets bright,
Wooden horses, wooden bricks,
Big fat lambs with fleeces white,
Dolls that smile and dolls that cry,
Soldiers ready for parade,
All are here for you to buy,
In this wonderful Arcade.

Toys are hanging up on strings,
Toys are laid in tempting rows,
And each shop with pretty things
Is so crammed it overflows.
Little girls and little boys
Oft are puzzled, we're afraid,
Which to choose of all the toys
In this wonderful Arcade.

'The New Eagle Kite, with traps, balls and bats,
German boxes of toys, and musical cats,
The game of Aunt Sally, an English farm,
And popguns from France that will do you no harm ...
So dear little friends, just bear this in mind,
'tis at H. PIEROTTI'S these wonders you'll find.' [1]

A VICTORIAN HANDBILL
If you enter a Toyshop, a
choice you behold,
Of articles pleasing, that
wait to be sold.
You have a variety,
choose where you will,
There are plenty
remaining for good
children still.

There was no television advertising in Victorian times. Instead, toymakers paid children to hand out printed sheets called handbills to people in the streets. These handbills contained verses advertising the latest games and inventions. The one above tempts you to visit the delights on show in the toyshop owned by H. Pierotti.

▶ Look inside a Victorian toyshop.

◀ Tackleton the toy merchant, with a jack-in-the-box.

An evil toy seller, Tackleton, is described by Charles Dickens in *The Cricket on the Hearth.*

'He was a domestic Ogre, who had been living on children all his life, and was their implacable enemy. He despised all toys ... [and sold] appalling masks; hideous, hairy, red-eyed Jacks in Boxes [and] Vampire Kites.' [2]

ROCKING HORSE

LEARNING TO BALANCE

The children hurry inside the toyshop and rush to the rocking horses. A little man peers over his paint-spattered glasses and asks in a whisper: 'What about this lovely dapple-grey horse? I carved it myself. It's just like one in Queen Victoria's own nursery!'

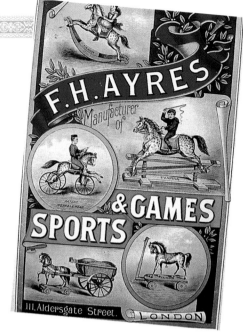

▶ You could buy all these horse toys in Harrods.

In Victorian times, boys were given balls, boats, train sets and model soldiers. Girls played with dolls, doll's houses, embroidery sets and model shops. This reflected their future roles in life. Both sexes, though, had rocking horses. Most were painted grey with dark spots, and had manes and tails of real horsehair. More expensive rocking horses were covered in real animal skin.

◀ Many children christened their rocking horse Dobbin.

▲ Two girls with a traditional rocking horse in 1860.

6

The first rocking horses stood on rockers, and were similar to babies' cradles. Riding them helped to give a child a sense of balance. If they were ridden too hard, horse and rider would topple over.

'Billy just breeched with conscious pride,
With joy the rocking horse must ride,
"Gee-up, gee-ho" – how fast he goes,
Till falling off, he breaks his nose;
In life we find 'tis so with all,
Who gallop fast may chance to fall.' [3]

With a head and a tail, ho, ho, ho, ho,
It's our legs which make him go.

▲ This beautiful horse chariot was made around 1895.

Some children pretended to ride on 'hobby horses', wooden sticks with a carved horse's head. Even more fun were horses on wheels which seemed to travel as fast as the real thing! The popularity of such toys reminds us how important horses were to the Victorians in the days before motor cars.

◀ A horse tricycle at full gallop in 1870.

LIFELIKE TOYS

The toy seller picks up the pieces of a broken doll and sighs: 'This was once a beautiful doll, with real hair. It was made by Pierotti and Montanari, the finest dollmakers in London. Now, she is just another guest in my doll's hospital.'

◀ This doll is a baby's rattle.

▶ A toyshop and doll's hospital.

The Victorians believed that playing with dolls taught a girl to become a good mother. Rich children had a selection of dolls. Flora Thompson in *Lark Rise to Candleford* remembers her May Day doll, which was taken from the toy cupboard only once a year. Expensive dolls had papier mâché heads covered in wax. They can be recognized today because the wax has cracked all over their faces.

'I once had a sweet little doll, dears!
The prettiest doll in the world.
Her cheeks were so red and so white, dears,
And her hair was so charmingly curled.
But I lost my poor little doll, dears,
As I played on the heath one day.
And I cried for her more than a week, dears,
But I never could find where she lay.' [4]

▼ Pedlar dolls selling their wares.

Some dolls show us popular Victorian occupations, such as servants and stable-boys. Home-made dolls like the ones on the right were dressed as 'pedlars', who travelled the country in Victorian times selling their many cheap goods.

Mechanical 'novelty dolls' were very lifelike. They could talk, cry, sing and swim. Three-faced dolls were popular, one of which combined the characters of Red Riding Hood, Grandmother and the Big Bad Wolf.

◀ A beautiful clockwork novelty doll.

Companion toy to Dollie Daisie Dimple, Quite new this season, A SAILOR BOY DOLL Romping, rollicking Roderick, With his sea chest, Containing three suits of clothes. ONE SHILLING.

Look inside a Victorian toyshop and you might see some unjointed dolls with a sinister, stiff appearance. These were called Frozen Charlottes after a folk song in which the heroine freezes to death.

▼ A mechanical walking doll.

THE PATENT AUTOPERIPATETIKOS WALKING-DOLL

*'Fair Charlotte was a frozen corpse
And her lips spake never more.'*[5]

◀ A poor London child's doll made from an old shoe.

▼ Miss Dollie Daisie Dimple, for sale in 1887.

Rich children had wax dolls with complete sets of fashionable clothes. A cheaper doll was Miss Dollie Daisie Dimple, who came with fifty articles of paper clothing for only a shilling. Poorer children made their own dolls which they could dress up, like the one above made from an old shoe.

DOLL'S HOUSE

MINIATURE HOMES

'This way!' cries the toy seller. At his workbench, an old man is building a miniature table from scraps of wood. He hands one of the girls a frying pan, no bigger than her thumbnail. She places it on a tiny kitchen stove, perfect in every detail. She then stands the little stove in the kitchen of the most beautiful doll's house she has ever seen.

▲ Two girls with their doll's house in 1862.

▼ An expensive doll's house, built in 1875.

▲ A doll's kitchen with stove and mangle.

If you look inside a Victorian doll's house, you can see what some real homes were like in the nineteenth century. The rooms are crowded with furniture and heated by coal fires, pictures hang on the walls, and the kitchen is stocked with crockery and food. There are attic rooms for the maids who cleaned, cooked, washed and looked after a rich family's children.

Furniture for doll's houses was made from wood, metal, glass, ivory, fishbones, even apple pips and conkers. Tiny pottery tea and dinner sets were made in factories by children working in dreadful conditions. A report written in 1842 tells of one poor nine-year-old, William Cotton, who worked seventy hours a week. He was paid the grand sum of two shillings for making nearly 3,000 pottery figures.

'Dolls' bedsteads', is my daily cry;
Ye misses, come and choose;
Such sorts and sizes I have here,
To buy you'll not refuse.

▶ A doll's teaset from the 1880s.

▼ Look inside the doll's house to see an even smaller doll's house!

In *The Cricket on the Hearth*, Dickens describes doll's houses made by a toymaker, called Caleb Plummer, and his blind daughter. The different miniature houses showed the difference between the real homes of rich and poor.

'There were houses ... for Dolls of all stations in life. Suburban tenements for Dolls of moderate means; kitchens and single apartments for Dolls of the lower classes; capital town residencies for Dolls of high estate.' 6

KNUCKLEBONES

PENNY TOYS

On display at the front of the shop is a selection of 'penny toys'. Two boys search their pockets for coins as they cast their eyes over skipping ropes, spinning tops, hoops, knucklebones, puppets and popguns. One of them sighs as he tries to choose between a 'plunker' and an 'alley' for his marble collection.

◀ A penny could buy this musical puppet.

▲ A box of spinning tops.

The toyseller kept penny toys for his poorer customers. Victorian children were just as lively as you are, and many cheap toys were made for street games. Spinning tops that whirred over flat surfaces were popular. Children became expert at spinning them by twisting the spindle between two fingers, whipping the top with a stick or throwing the top while holding its string.

▼ Many children played with hoops and sticks.

Girls bought skipping ropes with carved handles that played tinkling tunes. Glass marbles with dazzling colours were many boys' most prized possession, and they played fierce games to win them from each other. Poorer children, and poor players, had to make do with marbles made from nuts or hard berries.

▲ A jack-in-the-box to make you jump!

Come, my young masters, come to me, I've flags both red and blue; One penny is the price of them – My swords are well worth two.

▼ Two mice chase around this penny toy.

▶ Marbles were favourite toys in the schoolyard.

Jacks was a traditional throwing game, sometimes called knucklebones because the pieces were originally made from animal bones. There were also simple mechanical toys to tempt you to part with your shiny penny. A puppet that crashed two cymbals together seemed quite magical in days long before electronic toys.

▲ A box of knucklebones.

TRAINS

TRANSPORT TOYS

'That's more like it,' one boy shouts as he catches sight of a toy train. 'That's what I want for Christmas!' The toy seller chuckles and picks up the little locomotive. He winds a key in the engine's side, and sets it down on a track. The train dashes past a signal box, scoops up a bag of mail and vanishes into a dark tunnel.

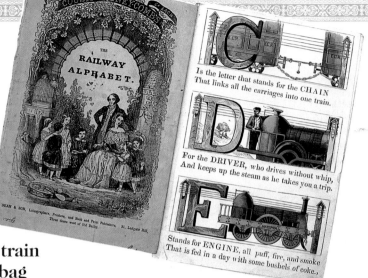

▲ A railway alphabet to help children learn their letters.

◀ Playing with a wooden cart in 1856.

Early Victorian toy vehicles were carts and barrows like the one shown here. The arrival of toy trains reminds us that the nineteenth century was the great railway age. George Stephenson's steam locomotive *Rocket* first ran in 1829, and children were buying toy trains less than fifteen years later.

The first wooden toy trains were pulled along, but those that really fired the imagination were working models of steam trains. These contained water-filled boilers heated by methylated spirit burners. They produced real smoke and could be quite dangerous.

◀ A wooden pull-along train.

◀ This toy train, made in Birmingham around 1860 and powered by methylated spirits, was called a Birmingham Dribbler.

Piggy on the railway, picking up stones. Up came an engine and broke Piggy's bones. 'Oh!' said Piggy, 'that's not fair.' 'Oh!' said the driver, 'I don't care.'

'Peter had a birthday present ... a model engine more perfect than you could ever have dreamed of ... Its charm lasted in its full perfection for exactly three days. Then ... the engine suddenly went off with a bang ... All the Noah's Ark people who were in the tender were broken to bits, but nothing else was hurt except the poor little engine and the feelings of Peter.' [7]

Clockwork trains that ran on rails became very popular. German manufacturers like Marklin used tin plate to produce cheap trains and accessories such as stations, engine sheds, signals and tunnels. An 1884 catalogue describes a more expensive locomotive with a brass boiler, copper back, bell and whistle, which could run 'backwards or forwards'.

▼ A tin-plate train set.

CLOCKWORK BEAR

MECHANICAL TOYS

The toy seller winds up a selection of mechanical animals. Soon, the children are staring in amazement at a dancing bear, a beetle flapping it wings, a bucking zebra and a cat playing a violin. Their favourite is an elephant that rolls its eyes, curls its trunk and wags its little tail!

◀ This clockwork man has to control a bucking zebra.

▲ If you wind up this Victorian toy bear, he rears up on his back legs.

Mechanical toys were known as 'automata'. They were sold quite cheaply by toyshops and street sellers. Many were models of figures playing instruments. They were usually operated by clockwork, the slow unwinding of a coiled spring. Victorian children did not play with cute, cuddly teddy bears, but with clockwork bears that looked quite lifelike and vicious!

◀ A girl with a selection of clockwork toys.

There were also simple mechanical toys. Acrobats like the one shown here turned flying somersaults when their handles were squeezed. 'Pantins' were little figures that lifted their arms and legs when their strings were pulled.

◀ A somersaulting acrobat.

Many automata were quite complicated and were really toys for adults. They were made in France, Germany or Switzerland, and could perform amazing actions, such as card tricks. Automata made by the French designer, Jacques de Vaucanson, were exhibited all over Europe. They included a flute player who performed twelve tunes.

▶ This clockwork, walking greyhound almost seems alive.

The Great Exhibition of 1851 gave a great boost to British toymaking. The exhibition was housed in the newly built Crystal Palace and featured a display of over 200,000 objects from all over the world, including toys from Britain and Europe. Many automata imitated the movements of animals, both domestic pets and the exotic species like monkeys, bears and zebras that were being shipped to British zoos from the growing Empire.

TOY SOLDIERS

WAR GAMES

Across the length of a table, a whole battalion of toy soldiers in freshly painted, cherry-red uniforms is marching into battle. One boy marches beside them, thinking about his own small box of soldiers and how much he would like to command this mighty army.

Winston Churchill, the British prime minister during World War II, had joined the army because of the toy soldiers he played with when growing up in the 1880s.

'I was now embarked on a military career ... due entirely to my collection of toy soldiers. I had ultimately nearly fifteen hundred. They were all of one size, all British, and organized as an infantry division with a cavalry brigade.' [8]

▲ These 'flats' of British soldiers were made in the 1840s.

The first metal toy soldiers, called 'flats', were flattened, tin figures with details on both sides. They were mostly made in Germany. Solid lead figures later became popular but were quite expensive. In the 1890s, a British toymaker called William Britain began producing cheaper boxed sets of light, hollow soldiers.

▲ William Britain soldiers including stretcher bearers, a nurse and a drummer boy.

◀ A brother and sister do battle in the 1850s.

William Britain's cheaper soldiers were soon fighting in many bedroom battlefields. Children could afford to recruit whole toy armies to fight war games with catapults, pea-shooters and marbles. Today, toy soldiers are often considered unsuitable toys for young children. In Victorian times, though, they meant that boys could dream about joining the British Army.

▼ A model of a Scottish soldier.

▲ A picture book celebrating the British Army.

▼ A cut-out figure of a Grenadier Guard.

The Army controlled a British Empire that covered a fifth of the world by Queen Victoria's death in 1901. The great detail of toy soldiers and accessories recorded the changing uniforms, weapons and transport used by Britain and her enemies' troops.

MAGIC LANTERN

MOVING PICTURES

A crowd gathers as the toy seller closes the shutters and plunges the toyshop into darkness. When everyone is seated in silence, he flicks the switch on his new magic lantern. Suddenly, a ghostly figure playing a guitar dances across the wall. The children gasp. It must be magic!

▶ A magic lantern and slides.

▲ A magic lantern show in 1884.

They even had horror films in Victorian times. In The Cricket on the Hearth, *Dickens describes how Tackleton the toy seller put on shows, using:*

'Goblin slides for magic-lanterns, whereon the Powers of Darkness were depicted as a sort of supernatural shell-fish, with human faces.' [9]

In the days before television, the magic lantern was a source of wonder. A candle or oil lamp illuminated glass slides painted with sequences of pictures. These might show a comic story, a nursery rhyme, or an educational subject such as the planets and stars.

Diabolical conjuring box containing sheet lightning, silver fire, pharaoh's serpent, Japanese fire, stars and limelight. Price: 1 Shilling.

▲ Spinning this 1882 phenakistoscope makes the horse appear to gallop.

Moving pictures were created in the 1830s by the 'phenakistoscope'. Figures painted on a cardboard disc appeared to come alive when spun quickly in front of a mirror. An improved version called the 'zoetrope' was known as the 'wheel of life' because of its lifelike images.

▲ Discs for a phenakistoscope.

▼ A praxinoscope made in 1880.

▼ The magic of a praxinoscope.

Inventions like the 'praxinoscope', which used a reel of pictures, led to the arrival of cinema in the 1890s. Some of today's special effects are based on the Victorian toymakers' use of lights and mirrors to create moving pictures.

TOY THEATRE

PUTTING ON A SHOW

A cluster of tiny, coloured lamps light up a finely painted toy theatre, in the doorway of the darkened shop. Its curtain shakily rises, to reveal cardboard figures on the stage of *Cinderella*. A tiny orchestra appears to play some music, before the figures start to move about, speaking in strange voices. The toy seller dashes about behind the theatre, puffing and blowing. He pulls the wires, plays the music, changes the lighting and speaks the characters' lines.

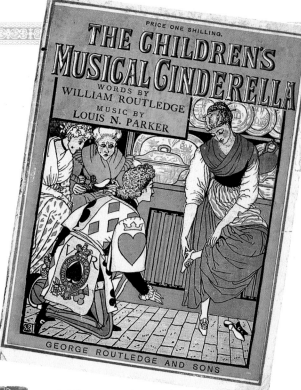

▲ The words and music for Cinderella.

Toy theatres were at their most popular in early Victorian times. They were miniature versions of real theatres, with working oil lamps, footlights, trapdoors and curtains. Cardboard actors and actresses were attached to long metal handles so that they could be moved around from behind the stage.

Each theatre was handmade by a craftsman. They were of such high quality that many survive in good condition today.

◀ A toy theatre from 1850, showing Little Red Riding Hood.

◀ A performance
of Cinderella in a
toy theatre.

The toy theatre was placed on a table in a
doorway screened by curtains, so that those
operating the characters could not be seen.
Children spent hours putting on a
performance. They could make up their own
plays, or use scripts that their parents had
bought for them.

Many Victorian publishers sold plays
written just for toy theatres. Some had
their own music, and notes directing the
entrances and exits of the figures. For
twopence, you could buy coloured
cardboard sheets with cut-out figures,
scenery and props. In 1835, there were
some thirty publishers producing plays
for toy theatres.

▶ A script and figures for Punch and Judy.

EDUCATIONAL TOYS

'**I** have the most marvellous dissected maps of every country in the world!' boasts the toy seller, pointing to some jigsaws. One girl complains: 'Those are the toys we're told to play with when our parents want us to be quiet. Father says there are times when children should be seen and not heard.'

◀ A 'dissected map' of Africa.

▲ Building blocks printed with the alphabet.

Victorian parents thought toys should be used for learning. The Great Exhibition had a huge educational section. Building blocks with a letter on each side taught children spelling and simple building skills. Older children built grand houses with the coloured blocks, pillars and arches of Dr. Richter's 'Anchor Boxes'. In 1897, Plasticine was invented for modelling. By the end of Victoria's reign, children were using the first Meccano sets to build models of another great Victorian invention – the motor car.

▶ Children have played with Plasticine since 100 years ago.

Jigsaw puzzles had been around since the 1760s. They were known as 'dissected maps' and were used to teach children geography. The poet William Cowper said that jigsaws had taught one four-year-old boy 'the situation of every kingdom, country, city, river and remarkable mountain in the world'.

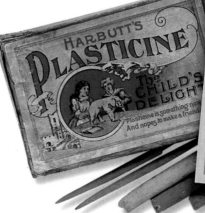

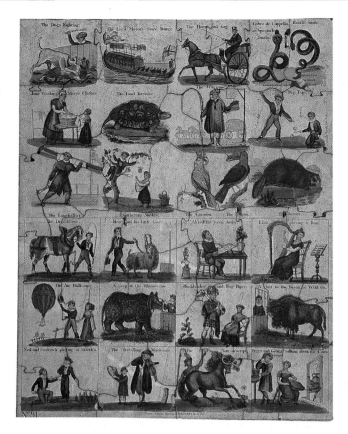

Take a look inside a Victorian toyshop and you will see jigsaws with pictures of Bible stories, nursery rhymes, railways and historical events like the explorer Henry Stanley's expedition to Africa. Jigsaws were used in schools, where children were told to: 'Fold up their work ... clean their slates ... and put the Dissected Maps in the proper Boxes.' [10]

▲ This jigsaw was made from 'scraps', sheets of coloured pictures sold for fourpence.

▼ Designs and bricks for Dr. Richter's Anchor Boxes.

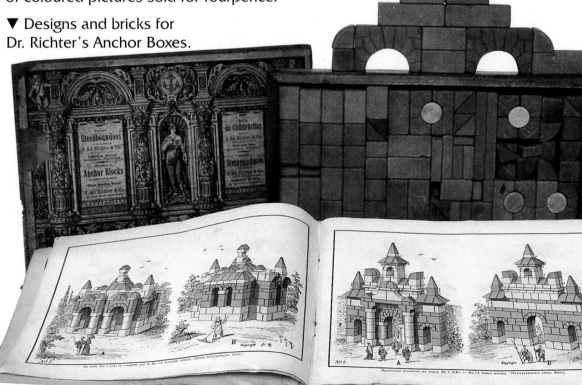

NOAH'S ARK

SUNDAY TOYS

The toyseller returns to painting a tiny pair of giraffes. On his workbench rests a hand-carved model of Noah's ark. Pairs of freshly painted animals are waiting to board it. 'Over one hundred of God's creatures, each carved and painted by myself,' he tells the children.

▼ Animals for an ark were painted in fine detail.

▲ Many Noah's arks have survived because they were only played with on a Sunday.

Noah's arks were known as Sunday toys. This was because many Victorian families thought it wrong to play on a Sunday unless it was with a toy that taught children about the Bible. If you lift up the roof of a Victorian ark and look inside, you will see a poem like the one below. It was written there by the toymaker, to tell the Bible story of Noah.

'The bad all died, but mark!
God saved good Noah's life.
He saved him in a mighty ark
With his three sons and wife,
And two of every kind
Of insect, beast and bird –
As He had said, for you will find
God always keeps his word.' [11]

Large arks contained amazingly detailed cats, dogs, moles, guinea pigs, birds; and insects including grasshoppers, ladybirds and butterflies with paper wings. Smaller sets might only contain Noah and his wife, with a dozen animals.

◀ A speaking book that made animal noises.

The Bible was usually read on Sundays, but there were more exciting children's books for sale in the toyshop. Some had pop-up characters and strings which made animal noises when pulled.

▶ Santa Claus, from a sheet of Christmas scraps.

Children also played with puzzles that had pictures from the Bible, and pasted bright pictures called scraps into books. In strict families, though, all toys were forbidden on a Sunday. It must have seemed a very long day for some children. Perhaps they spent it dreaming of their next visit to the toyshop!

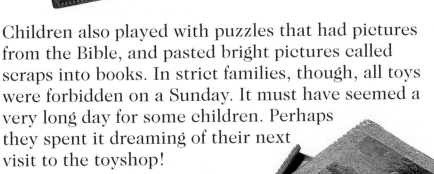

◀ A religious puzzle to play with on a Sunday.

SPILLIKINS

FAMILY GAMES

A boy and girl enter the toyshop with their parents and kick the snow from their shoes. 'I want that train set,' the boys cries. 'We need some new games,' shouts his sister. Their father winks at the toyseller. 'It's nearly Christmas, so you'll have to wait and see. I'll call back later ... on my own!'

▲ This lotto set used pictures instead of numbers.

Many Victorian games are still played today. Pin the tail on the donkey, Happy Families and Lotto (now called Bingo) were all popular. Board games included horse races around an oval track marked with hedges and water jumps.

One Victorian game of morals was called 'Virtue Rewarded and Vice Punished'. Snakes and Ladders boards also carried moral messages, with one snake carrying you down from 'Bad Temper' to 'Murder'.

◄ A Victorian game of lotto, which is played like the National Lottery – without the prizes!

▲ A pack of Happy Families cards.

He opens his eyes
with a cry of delight,
There's a toyshop
all round him,
a wonderful sight!
The fairies have
certainly called
in the night.

▼ Spillikins required
a steady hand.

In 'spillikins' or 'pick up sticks', children tried to slide coloured sticks from a pile without disturbing any others. Sets were made from bone, ivory or boxwood in the shape of tools and weapons, but children also played the game with used matches.

▼ A Christmas game of Happy Families.

In the days before television, games were a vital part of family life. The Victorians believed play should be educational, but toys and games were also a great source of enjoyment and entertainment that the whole family could share.

GLOSSARY

Accessories Small, extra items, such as a toy soldier's weapons.

Aunt Sally A model of a woman's head used as a target in fairground games.

Automata Mechanical toys that move.

Battalion A large unit of soldiers.

British Empire Parts of the world once ruled by Britain.

Catalogue A list of items for sale.

Dissected Cut up into pieces.

Footlights Lights set in a row along a theatre stage.

Great Exhibition A display of inventions and machines held in 1851.

Implacable Unable to be made peaceful.

Jack-in-the-box A toy figure that springs from its box.

Jacks A throwing game.

Locomotive A powered engine used for pulling trains.

Methylated Spirits A substance made from alcohol that is highly inflammable.

Morals The knowledge of right and wrong.

Noah's ark The ship, in the Bible story, built by Noah to save his family and the animals from the Flood.

Ogre A fierce flesh-eating giant.

Optical Making use of light.

Popguns Toy guns that use air to fire a cork, making a 'pop' sound.

Props Items used on a stage.

Spindle A pin or axis about which something turns.

Suburban On the edge of a city.

Tenements Large houses divided into rooms for rent.

Tricycle A three-wheeled cycle.

Sabbath Sunday, the day of rest for Christians.

FURTHER READING

BOOKS TO READ

Chrisp, Peter *History of Toys and Games* (Wayland, 1996)

Deary, Terry *The Vile Victorians* (Hippo, 1994)

Dickens, Charles *The Cricket on the Hearth* (1843)

Faulkner, Simon & Lucy *A Victorian Sunday* (Wayland, 1994)

Flick, Pauline *Old Toys* (Shire, 1995)

Kalman, Bobbie & Schimpky, David *Old Time Toys* (Crabtree 1995)

Oxlade, Chris *Toys Through Time* (Macdonald Young, 1995)

Siliprandi, Katrina *Victorian Toys and Games* (Wayland, 1994)

Guidebook to The Museum of Childhood, Edinburgh

Guidebook to Pollock's World of Toys, London

QUOTES FROM THE TOYSHOP

1. A nineteenth-century handbill, quoted in *History of Toys and Games*, Peter Chrisp.

2. *The Cricket on the Hearth*, Charles Dickens.

3. A popular poem dating from 1799.

4. *The Water Babies*, Charles Kingsley, 1863.

5. A traditional folk song.

6. *The Cricket on the Hearth*, Charles Dickens.

7. *The Railway Children*, Edith Nesbit, 1906.

8. Winston Churchill quoted in *Model Soldiers*, Henry Harris (Octopus, 1962).

9. *The Cricket on the Hearth*, Charles Dickens.

10. A tutor in 1826 quoted in *The English Jigsaw Puzzle*, Linda Hannas (Wayland, 1972).

11. Verse from a Noah's Ark quoted in *Playthings Past*, Betty Cadbury (David & Charles, 1976).

VICTORIAN MONEY:

1 pound = 20 shillings

1 shilling = 12 pennies

1 penny = 2 halfpennies

1 halfpenny = 2 farthings

Numbers in **bold** refer to pictures.